Green Day

Play Along with 8 Great-Sounding Tracks

`MW01152402`

Contents

Alfred Publishing Co., Inc.
16320 Roscoe Blvd., Suite 100
P.O. Box 10003
Van Nuys, CA 91410-0003
alfred.com

ISBN-10: 0-7390-4431-1 (Book & CD)
ISBN-13: 978-0-7390-4431-5 (Book & CD)

CD recorded at the Mews Recording Studios, London
www.themewsrecordingstudios.com
Dave Clarke, recording & mix engineer
Tom Fleming, guitars
Neil Williams, bass
Darrin Mooney, drums
Elysian String Quartet, strings

Book edited by Lucy Holliday & Olly Weeks
Music arranged & engraved by Tom Fleming

Cover photograph: © Peter Still/Redferns

AMERICAN IDIOT

Words by BILLIE JOE
Music by GREEN DAY

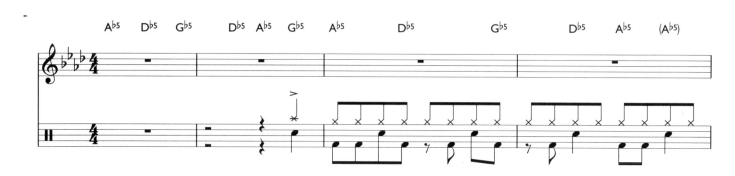

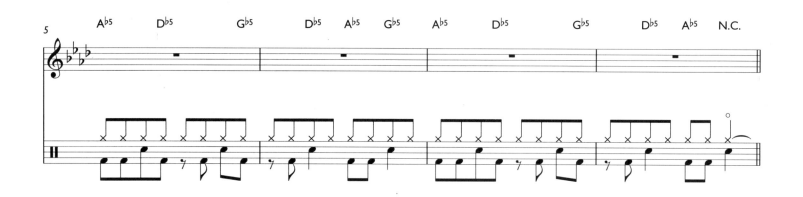

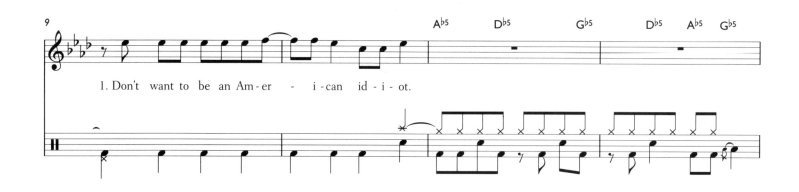

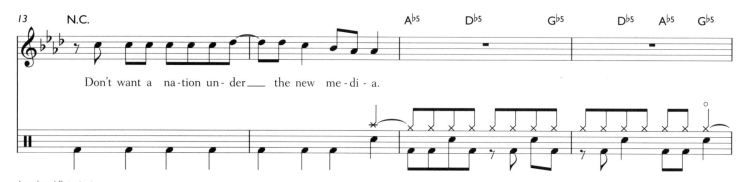

American Idiot - 6 - 1
26322

To Coda ⊕
To Coda ⊕⊕

for that's en-ough to ar-gue.

2. Well may-be I'm the fag - got Am-er-i-ca.

I'm not a part of a red-neck a-gen-da.

Now ev-'ry-bo-dy, do the pro-pa-gan-da,

and sing a - long in the age___ of pa - ra - noi - a.

⊕ *Coda*

(HH half open)

(Guitar solo)

Don't want to be an Am - er -

BASKET CASE

Words by BILLIE JOE
Music by GREEN DAY

1. Do you have the time___ to lis-ten to me whine___ a-

-bout noth-ing and ev-'ry-thing___ all at___ once?

I___ am one of those___ me-lo-dra-ma-tic fools;___ neu-

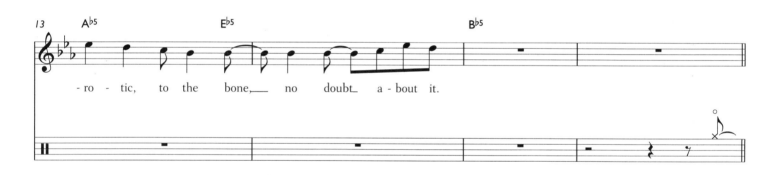

-ro-tic, to the bone,___ no doubt___ a-bout it.

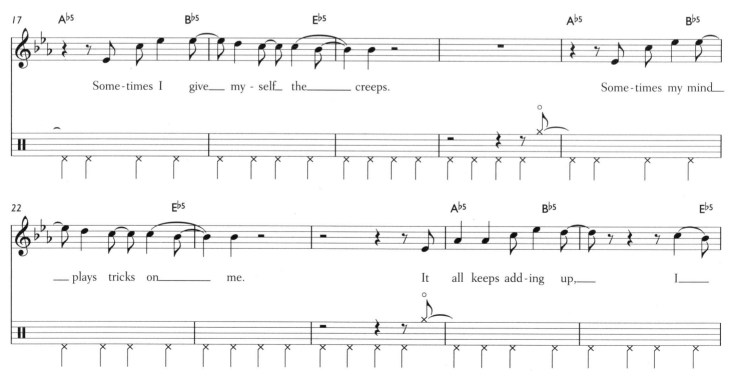

Some-times I give___ my-self_ the___ creeps. Some-times my mind___

___plays tricks on___ me. It all keeps add-ing up,___ I___

Basket Case - 5 - 1
26322

BOULEVARD OF BROKEN DREAMS

Words by BILLIE JOE
Music by GREEN DAY

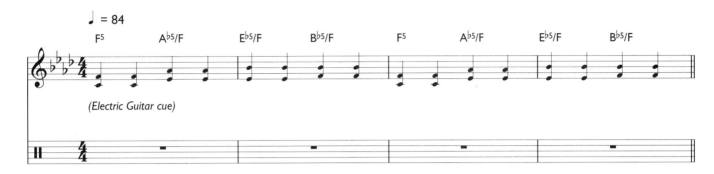

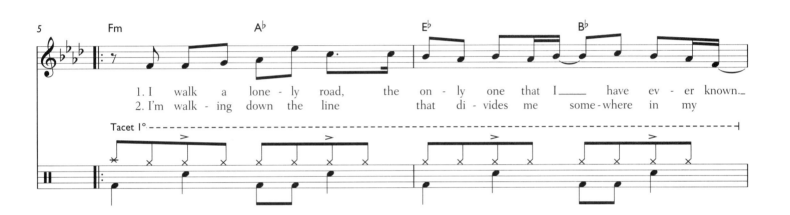

1. I walk a lone-ly road, the on-ly one that I___ have ev-er known.___
2. I'm walk-ing down the line that di-vides me some-where in my

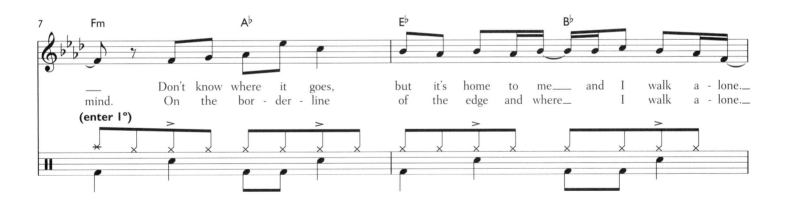

___ Don't know where it goes, but it's home to me___ and I walk a-lone.___
mind. On the bor-der-line of the edge and where___ I walk a-lone.___

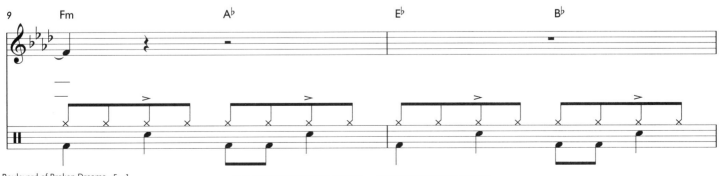

Boulevard of Broken Dreams - 5 - 1
26322

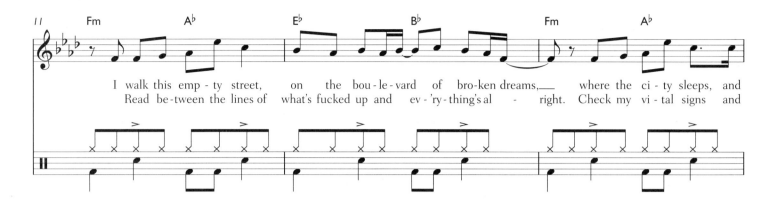

I walk this emp - ty street, on the bou - le - vard of bro - ken dreams,___ where the ci - ty sleeps, and
Read be - tween the lines of what's fucked up and ev - 'ry - thing's al - right. Check my vi - tal signs and

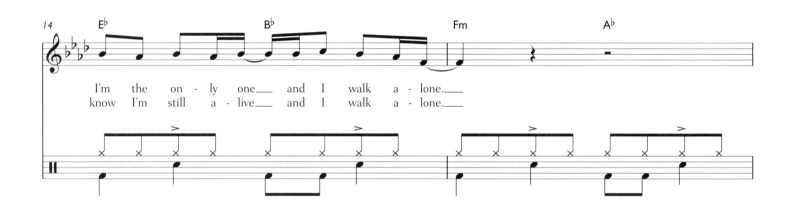

I'm the on - ly one___ and I walk a - lone.___
know I'm still a - live___ and I walk a - lone.___

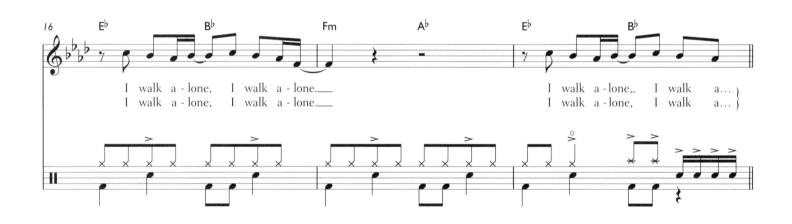

I walk a - lone, I walk a - lone.___ I walk a - lone, I walk a...
I walk a - lone, I walk a - lone.___ I walk a - lone, I walk a...

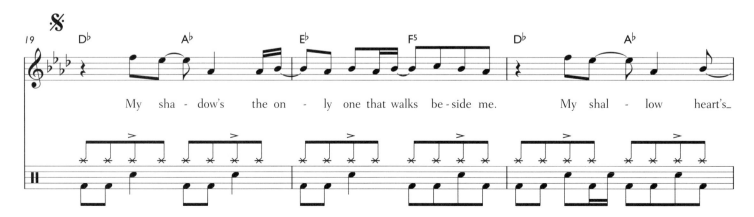

My sha - dow's the on - ly one that walks be - side me. My shal - low heart's_

To Coda ⊕

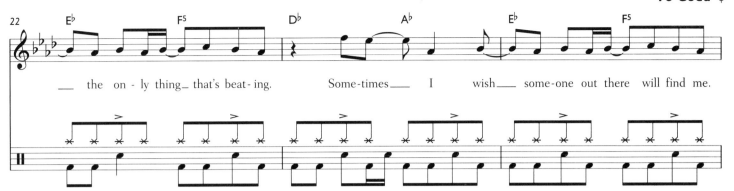

the on - ly thing that's beat - ing. Some-times___ I wish___ some-one out there will find me.

'Til then___ I walk___ a - lone.___ Ah, ___ ah, ___

ah, ___ ah, ___ ah, ___ ah, ___ ah. ___

a - lone.___ Ah, ___ ah, ___ ah, ___ ah, ___

Boulevard of Broken Dreams - 5 - 3
26322

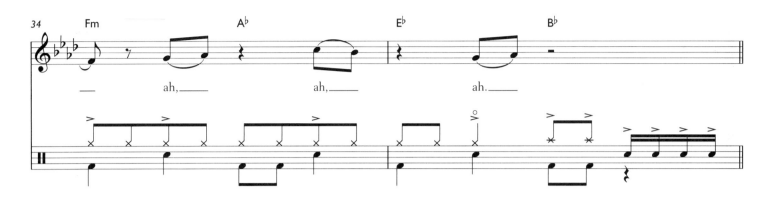

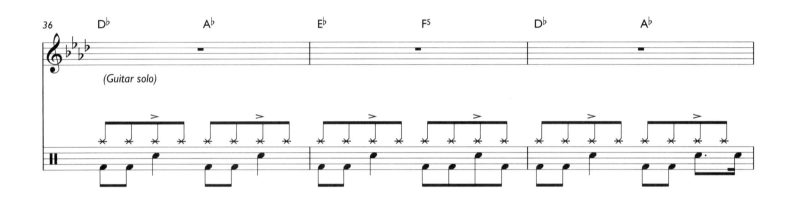

(Guitar solo)

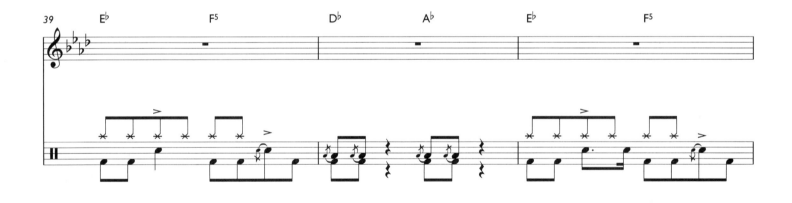

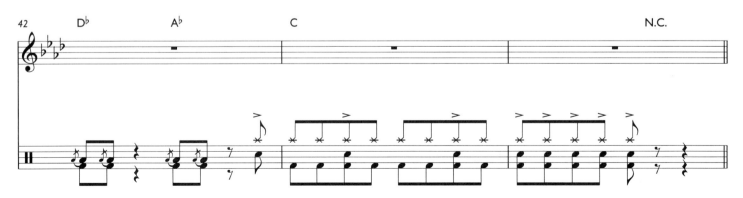

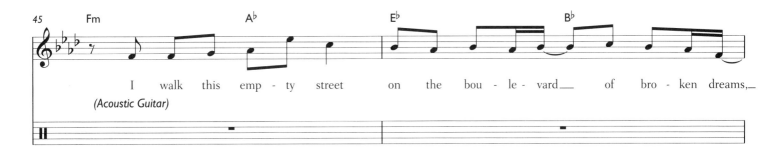

I walk this emp-ty street on the bou-le-vard___ of bro-ken dreams,___

(Acoustic Guitar)

D.%al Coda

___ where the ci-ty sleeps, and I'm the on-ly one,___ and I walk a...

Coda

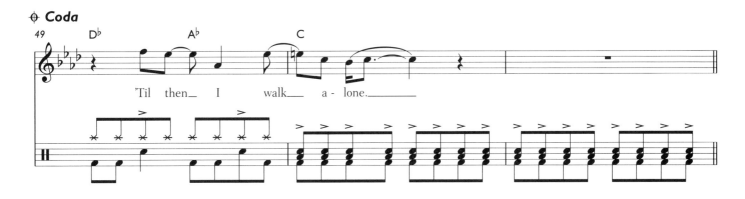

'Til then___ I walk___ a - lone._____

BRAIN STEW

Words by BILLIE JOE
Music by GREEN DAY

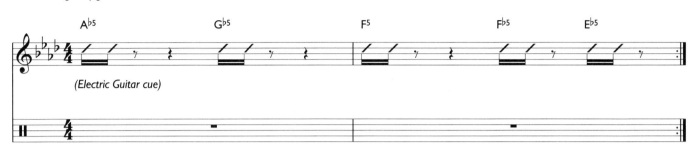

(Electric Guitar cue)

1. I'm hav-ing trou-ble try-ing to sleep.
2. My eyes feel like they're gon-na bleed,
3. My mind is set on ov-er-drive.

(HH closed)

Tacet 1°- -

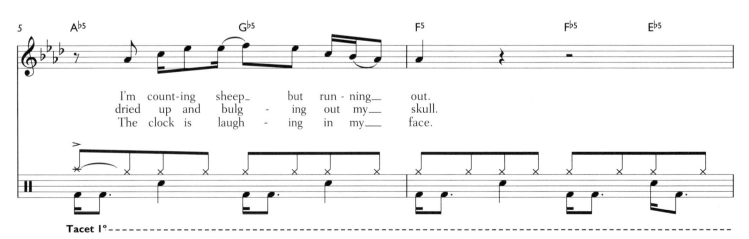

I'm count-ing sheep but run-ning out.
dried up and bulg - ing out my skull.
The clock is laugh - ing in my face.

Tacet 1°- -

Brain Stew - 4 - 1
26322

20

4. My eyes feel like__ they're gon - na bleed,__

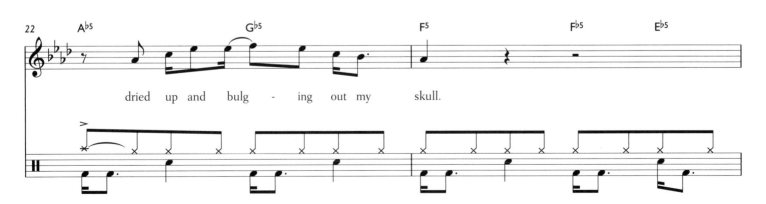

dried up and bulg - ing out my skull.

Brain Stew - 4 - 3
26322

LONGVIEW

Words by BILLIE JOE
Music by GREEN DAY

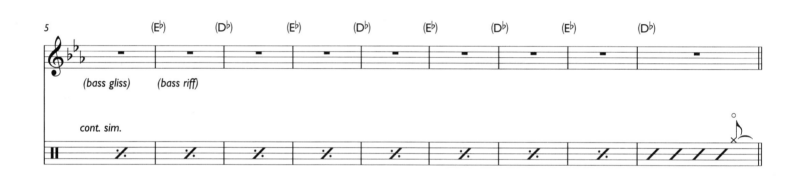

(bass gliss)   (bass riff)

cont. sim.

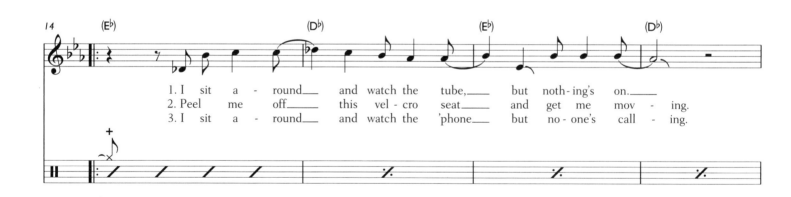

1. I sit a-round___ and watch the tube,___ but noth-ing's on.___
2. Peel me off___ this vel-cro seat___ and get me mov - ing.
3. I sit a-round___ and watch the 'phone___ but no-one's call - ing.

I change the chan-nels for an hour___ or___ two,___
I sure as hell___ can't do it by___ my-self.___
Call me pa - thet - ic, call me what___ you___ will.___

Longview - 4 - 1
26322

24

Longview - 4 - 3
26322

MINORITY

Words by BILLIE JOE
Music by GREEN DAY

2 bars count in

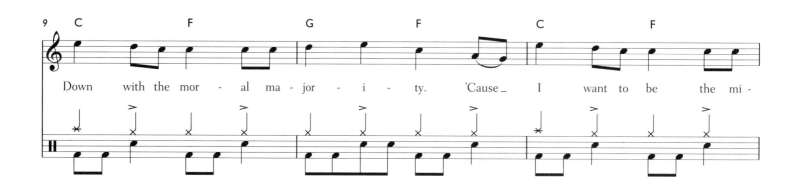

(Acoustic Guitar)

I want to be the mi - nor - i - ty. I don't _ need your au - thor - i - ty.

(HH half open)

Down with the mor - al ma - jor - i - ty. 'Cause _ I want to be the mi -

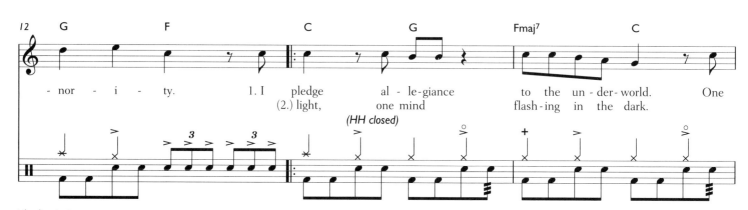

- nor - i - ty. 1. I pledge al - le - giance to the un - der - world. One
(2.) light, one mind flash - ing in the dark.

(HH closed)

28

Minority - 4 - 3
26322

Minority - 4 - 4
26322

WHEN I COME AROUND

Words by BILLIE JOE
Music by GREEN DAY

When I Come Around - 4 - 4
26322

WAKE ME UP WHEN SEPTEMBER ENDS

Words by BILLIE JOE
Music by GREEN DAY

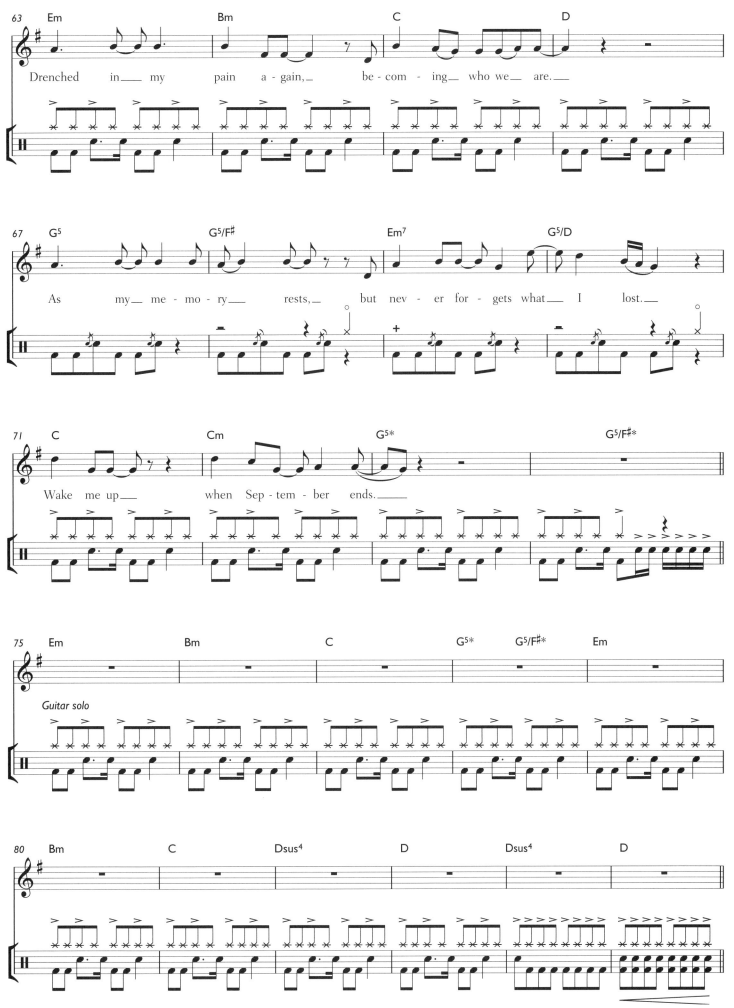

Drum Notation Guide

General Notation

Drum music is written on a standard five-line stave. You will see a neutral clef, or no clef, at the start of each stave. Occasionally, bass or treble clefs are used.

Neutral clef   Treble clef   Bass clef

Repeat Bars and Slash Notation

This sign [✗] indicates that the previous bar is repeated.
Numbered bars are used to help you count through a section.

The two-bar repeat means that the previous two bars are repeated.

Slash notation means "continue in the same style," with any fills or other changes to the pattern notated as they occur.

Notation for Drums

Bass Drum   Snare Drum   Toms: 2-Tom Setup   Toms: 3-Tom Setup   Toms: 4-Tom Setup

Roll Notation

Normally played as a buzz roll—each stick buzzes against the drum head.

Flam

Two notes very close together, played with different sticks

Flam between two different drums

Written   Played

Drag

Two grace notes before the beat (played with the same stick) and a main note (with the other stick)

Larger grace-note groups, for example

r r L
l l R

(R = play note with the right-hand stick; L = play with the left-hand stick)

40

Paradiddle

A common sticking pattern

R L R R L R L L R L R R L R L L

Play on Rim of Drum

Cymbals

Ride Cymbal   Crash Cymbal
(RC)   (CC)

Closed Hi-Hat Open Hi-Hat
(HH)

Open hi-hat notes are usually played just slightly open, so that the cymbals "sizzle" together. Play the hi-hats with the edge of the stick to accent these notes.

Hi-Hat with Foot   Closed Hi-Hat
                    (written after an open note)

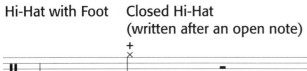

The + sign shows when to close the hi-hats if there is no note played. For example:

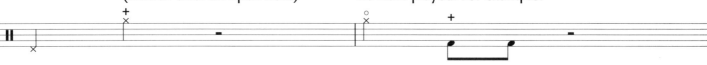

Let cymbal ring   Choke Cymbal:
                       play cymbal, then immediately
                       stop it from ringing.

General Points

Accented notes: play louder than others.

Other Instruments

Cowbell